Why Do I Pee When I Sneeze? A Picture Book For Women Over the Age of 40.

Printed in the United States of America by IngramSpark

Cataloguing-in-Publication data is available from the Library of Congress.

Schultz, Larissa J., Why Do I Pee When I Sneeze? A Picture Book For Women Over the Age of 40 SUMMARY: Advice in rhyme for women dealing with the challenges of aging in a world trying to balance vanity and depth of character.

ISBN: 978-0-9991582-2-7

10 9 8 7 6 5 4 3 2 1

For Liska

Why do I pee when I sneeze?
This truly makes me displeased.

What is that hair growing out of my chin?

Where did it come from?

Somewhere within?

What is that flab when I hail for a cab?

Why is it there?

Why do I care?

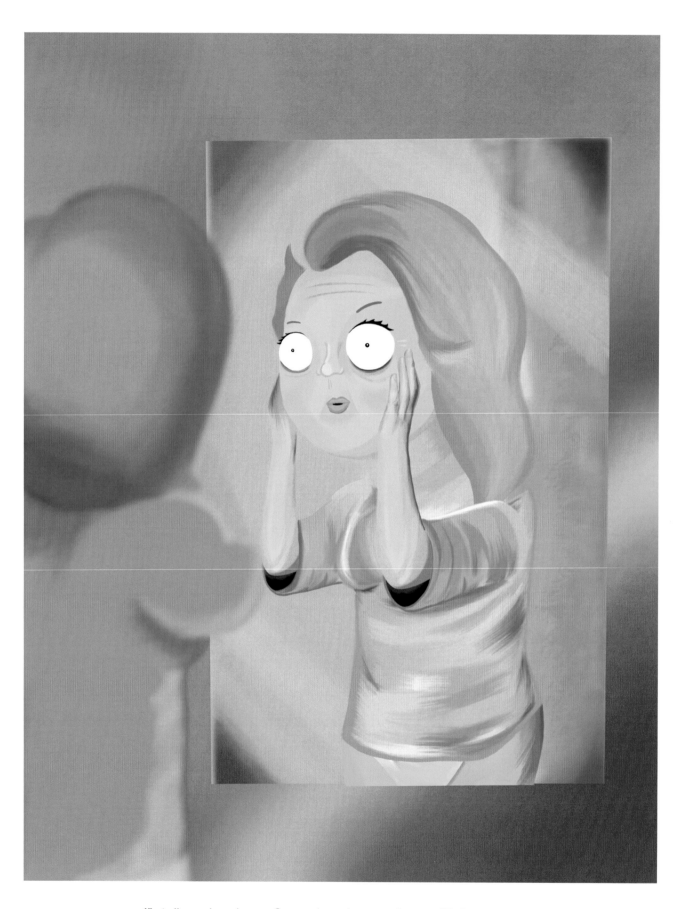

"Who is that face in the mirror?" I moan.
The wrinkles, the crinkles, the dryness, the tone.

Oh, how the years have flown by.
with friends and family, I know I can't lie...

.....but how can it be, that my younger me,

has grown up dreading my ass —

that keeps spreading?

Yes, that's what I'll do! That's what I need!

Fill my glass to the rim with a ruby red Zin!

In the morning I'll see it was all a bad dream!

EEEEKKKK!!!!!

It is dawn. And the wrinkles aren't gone.
The line in the sand has been drawn!

Now for the newest, ever greatest, get the latest!
Anti-wrinkle, anti-crinkle,
anti-aging, dark spot fading,
brightener, lightener, ever tight-ener,
smoother, straight-ener,
anti-puffin'.....

Two months have gone by.
My drawers and my cupboards are filled to the brim
with lotions and potions, scrubs and rubs,
ointments and creams.
It is all too much, it makes me just scream!

The fountain of youth was here I just knew it.

In 6-8 weeks, my face was to prove it.

The serums, the salves, the powders, and potions,

the opinions, the comments, the gossip, the notions.

Belie life's meaning, our purpose, our mission;

to live life to the fullest despite our condition.

Hair dye may cover the age of a mother,
but her wisdom and purpose will not be smothered.
The strength and substance, the weight of her worth,
is seen in her actions and words;
not her face or her girth.

So.....

    ...maybe my hair has gone thin,

    and there is a slight sag in my chin.

    My nose keeps growing, my eyelashes going.

    My belly distending, my breasts descending.

But the bumps and the bruises

    show the tried and the trueness,

      of a life well lived, well loved, and well worn.

And my memories and stories of old days of glory,
fill my mind and my head with good things
not dread.

For my heart holds true, the empowering support,
the love and the unity of this community.
And the strength and the smiles...
...yes, the strength and the smiles...

...seen marching across all those miles.

The End

For Now...

Special Acknowledgements

Special Thanks to those social media friends who took my random musing, one day 4 years ago, and fed on it. Instilling in me the thought that this laughable moment could create into something larger. Thanks Michelle, Lisa, TJ, Bronya, Angie, Joni, LeAnn, Christina, Rebecca, Princess Lisa, Lauren, Monica, Brian, and Christine.

Scott Barnes—my friend, my lover, my heart. You amaze me everyday with your continued support and belief in me.

My wild, wacky women who keep me real, keep me humble, keep me sane, and bring a smile to my face - your friendship has blessed my life and my soul.

To those who gave of their time and talent providing insight and input and helping generate this idea into the living, breathing instrument it is today. Your time is greatly appreciated.

To Max, your enthusiasm for this project helped to keep me going and your talent brought us the woman we needed. I hope your mother really likes it!

And to all the women, and the men who support women, who continue to strive, overcome obstacles - both literal and figurative - who continue to believe in themselves and each other, and know there is more for yourself, for each of us, and the greatness of us.

#keepmovingforward

#bekind

CPSIA information can be obtained
at www.ICGtesting.com
Printed in the USA
LVXC01n1950151117
556283LV00003B/5